THIS IS GOD'S WORLD

THIS IS GOD'S WORLD

Songs of praise and possibility

John L. Bell
The Wild Goose Resource Group

WILD GOOSE PUBLICATIONS

First published in 2021
copyright © 2021 Wild Goose Resource Group, Iona Community, Glasgow, Scotland.
www.wildgoose.scot

ISBN 978-1-84952-786-6

Published by Wild Goose Publications,
Suite 9, Fairfield, 1048 Govan Road, Glasgow G51 4XS, Scotland
the publishing division of the Iona Community.
Scottish Charity No. SC003794. Limited Company Reg. No. SC096243.
www.ionabooks.com

John L. Bell/The Wild Goose Resource Group have asserted their rights under the Copyright, Designs and Patents Act, 1988, to be identified as the authors of this work.

The authors and Wild Goose Publications wish to thank all who have given permission for songs to be included in this collection. We have made every effort to trace and identify the authors and copyright holders correctly, and to secure all the necessary permissions for reprinting. Copyright acknowledgements can be found at the foot of the music for each song.

All rights reserved. No part of this publication may be reproduced commercially in any form or by any means without permission from the copyright holders. Information on non-commercial reproduction can be found at www.wildgoose.scot/copyright.

A catalogue record for this book is available from the British Library.

Distributed in Australia by Willow Publishing Pty Ltd, PO Box 1061, Dee Why NSW 2099, Australia, and in New Zealand by Pleroma Christian Supplies, Higginson St., Otane, Central Hawkes Bay 4202, New Zealand. Permission to reproduce any part of this work in Australia or New Zealand should be sought from Willow Publishing.

Published in North America by GIA Publications, Inc., 7404 South Mason Avenue, Chicago, IL 60638, USA. Permission to reproduce any part of this work in the USA or Canada should be sought from GIA Publications, Inc.

Cover design by Jo Love, from original artwork by Graham Maule,
copyright © 2021 Wild Goose Resource Group, Iona Community, Glasgow, Scotland.

Music origination by Josh Harvey
copyright © 2021 Wild Goose Resource Group, Iona Community, Glasgow, Scotland.

Printed by Bell & Bain, Glasgow, Scotland.

To the memory of the unforgettable
Graham Maule
1958–2019

friend
fellow traveller
faithful witness

Contents

9	Introduction

The Songs

12	This is the day
16	All people living on the earth
20	What is this place?
24	In Christ we live
28	Long have you loved me
30	There is a balm – *African-American*
34	Now we are nourished
38	Lord Jesus, I'm eager to answer your call
40	The Lord of the earth
46	This is God's world
50	God give them peace
54	We are coming, Lord, to the table – *Sierra Leone*
58	Within the circle of your friends
62	God and parent of all people
66	God loved the world so much
70	Go, heal the sick
76	Murassala – *South Sudan*
78	Canticle of the turning
82	I lie down with God
87	Alphabetical index of first lines

Introduction

This collection should have been published over a year ago, but the sudden illness and untimely death of our friend and colleague Graham Maule meant that the best laid plans could not be fulfilled.

Among so many other things, Graham was the project manager. He organised the CD recording which accompanies this book; he scrutinised the text; he was part way through setting the music. And as with other collections, he would have designed and illustrated the book and CD, registered the songs with the relevant authorities, drawn up contracts with copyright holders and and signed off the final digital files for the printer.

But that was not to be. So I am deeply grateful to our administrator Gail Ullrich for picking up more pieces than I can imagine, to my colleague Jo Love who searched lovingly through Graham's doodles to find and modify one as the cover design, and to both for their painstaking proofing.

I am grateful too to Iain McLarty who rehearsed and conducted the singers and musicians, most of whom had never sung with each other before. He also generously involved others – particularly Margaret McLarty, Phill Mellstrom and Richard Michael – in arranging and sometimes improvising the music. These are the principal 'others' who appear from time to time in the credits. Thanks also to Josh Harvey on the other side of the Atlantic, coming to our aid in typesetting and formatting the music as well as making tasteful contributions to accompaniments.

Like our other collections, this is intentionally a mixed bag. There are tunes that come from different parts of the world, two of which Iain became aware of when working at the World Council of Churches' 2018 Conference in Tanzania. There are a few traditional texts, but most are original. The sequence of songs roughly mirrors the flow of worship – gathering, hearing the word, responding and leaving.

We have frequently been asked for the genesis of a song, and just as frequently Graham and I said little by way of reply. Perhaps it has been an over-exposure to singer-songwriters who have spent ten minutes in concerts explaining what delight or disaster befell them which caused them to write the lyrics 'which I'm going to sing for you now'. For us a song – if it is intended for public sharing – should not be authenticated by the history of its conception, but by whether the participating singers and listeners can give it their Amen. This is the secret behind the Psalms. Written by who knows whom (certainly not King David) over three thousand years ago, we can only guess why. What is more important is that they speak of God to us and of us to God.

However, as two of the songs developed from specific and unusual situations, we have made a brief mention of the background story.

None of these songs are 'new' or specially written for this collection. Most have been hiding in scrawny manuscript form for several years, and subject to occasional revision.

But four have been previously recorded in full choral versions by the Cathedral Singers of Chicago; details below.

That's enough by way of introduction. We fondly dedicate these songs to Graham's memory. He sang them on earth and will sing them with us from heaven.

John L. Bell
The Wild Goose Resource Group
September 2020

The following have been published as choral anthems by GIA Publications, Inc., Chicago.

All People Living on the Earth	G-8011
Canticle of the Turning	G-3407
In Christ We Live	G-8018
The Lord of the Earth	G-8020
There is a Balm	G-5170

In the UK, they are available from The Wild Goose Resource Group as part of the collections **The Splendour of the House of God** and **Take This Moment** – www.wildgoose.scot

In North America they are available from the publisher – www.giamusic.com

The songs in this collection have been recorded by the Wild Goose Collective on a CD of the same title.

The songs

This is the day

Words & Music: John L. Bell
Tune: LENBEO

Words & Music copyright © 2020 WGRG, Iona Community, Glasgow, Scotland. www.wildgoose.scot

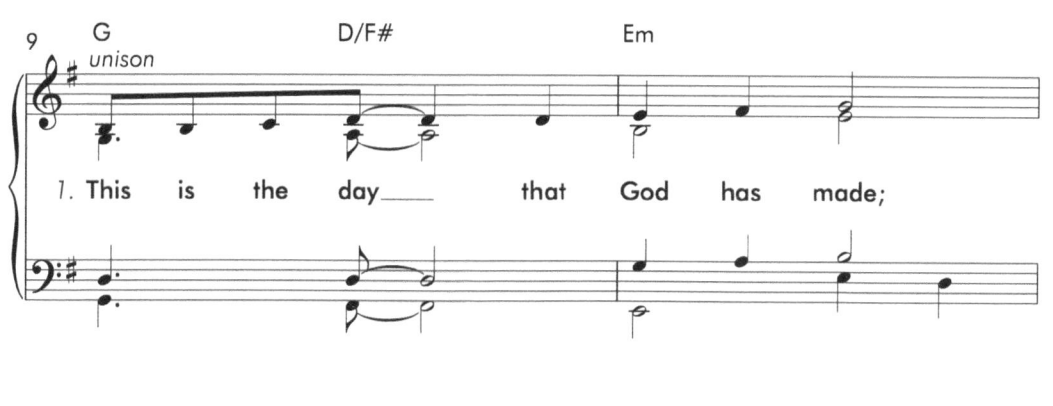

Hallelujah! Hallelujah! Hallelujah! Hallelujah!
Hallelujah! Hallelujah! Hallelujah! Hallelujah!

1. This is the day that God has made;
   grace, truth and beauty are displayed.
   No day will ever be the same
   so let's praise God's holy name:

2. This is the day when we can see
   God's passion for diversity:
   colour and culture, landscape, race,
   different contours, each in place.

3. This is the day when we may find
   nourishment for both soul and mind:
   insights and wisdom, calls to care,
   food enough for faith and prayer.

4. This is the day in which we know
   kindness and love are meant to grow:
   love to the stranger, to the friend,
   to the world – love without end.

5. This is the day we will rejoice,
   stretch our horizons, raise our voice,
   join in earth's symphony of love
   improvised for heaven above.

An alternative second verse for use on Sundays

2. This is the day God meant for rest
   through which the world and we are blessed:
   rest from our work and all we crave,
   rest from all that can enslave.

As with many songs of this type, there is no need to encourage exhaustion by requiring all to sing every verse. Solo voices, a choir or singing group, men and women, or different sections of the congregation can be invited to sing different verses, and everyone joins in the chorus.

All people living on the earth

Paraphrase of Psalm 100 & Arrangement: John L. Bell
Melody: Swee Hong Lim

Paraphrase & Arrangement copyright © 2011, 2020 WGRG, Iona Community, Glasgow, Scotland. www.wildgoose.scot
Melody copyright © 2000 Swee Hong Lim, administered by the General Board of Global Ministries t/a GBGMusik.

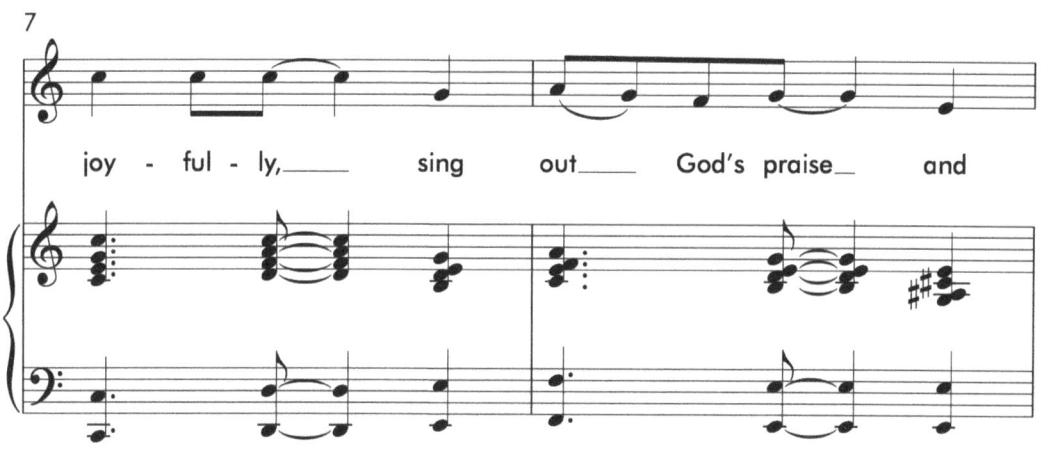

17

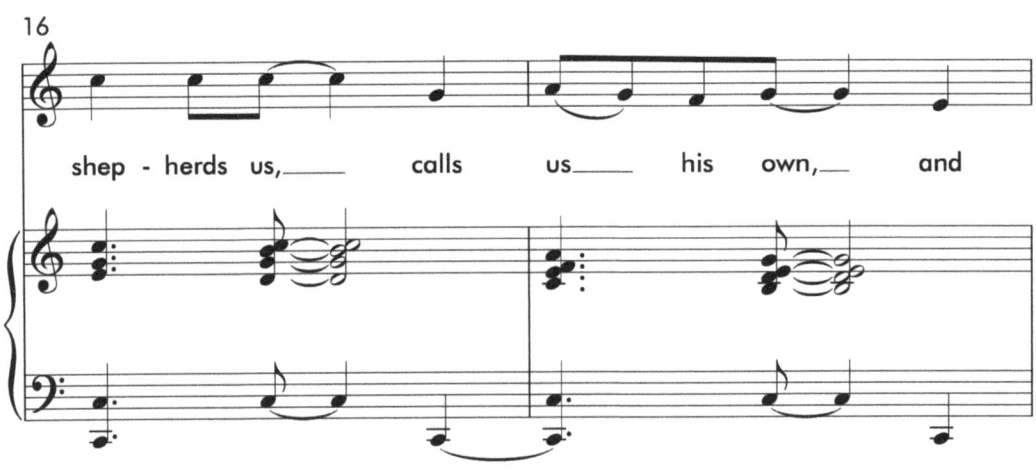
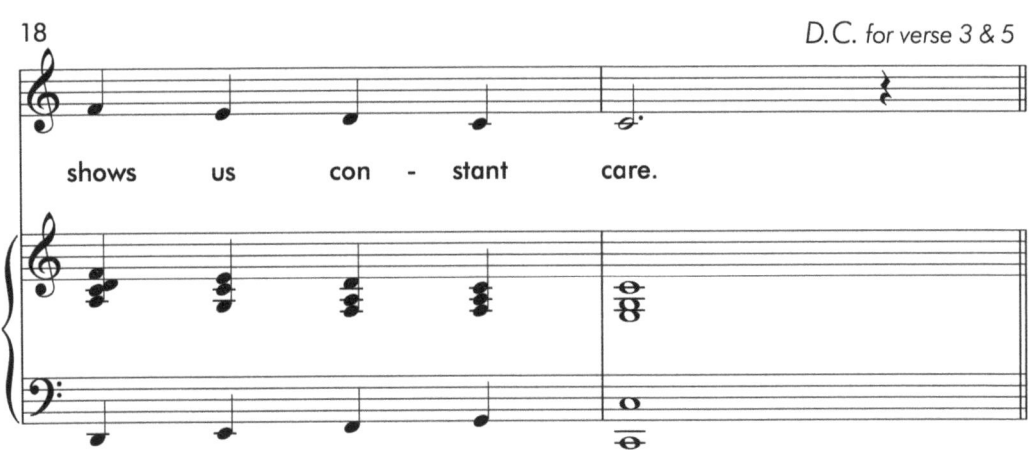

1. All people living on the earth,
   sing to the Lord with cheerful voice;
   serve joyfully, sing out God's praise
   and in this place rejoice.

2. Know that the Lord is God indeed
   whose parenting is firm and fair;
   God shepherds us, calls us his own
   and shows us constant care.

3. Where we now stand is heaven's gate,
   so enter in with songs of praise;
   give thanks and bless God's holy name
   in endless words and ways.

4. For God is good, God's love shall last;
   God's faithfulness is always sure;
   to generations yet unborn
   God's kindness will endure.

5. Amen! Amen! Alleluia!
   Let praise to God be given.
   Amen! Amen! Alleluia!
   Let earth be one with heaven.

This paraphrase of Psalm 100 is set to a tune by the Singaporean-Chinese composer Swee Hong Lim who is now a professor in Emmanuel College, Toronto, teaching primarily in the areas of music in worship and global hymnody.

A choral arrangement of this song is available. See introduction for details.

What is this place?

Words & Music: John L. Bell
Tune: CAUSER

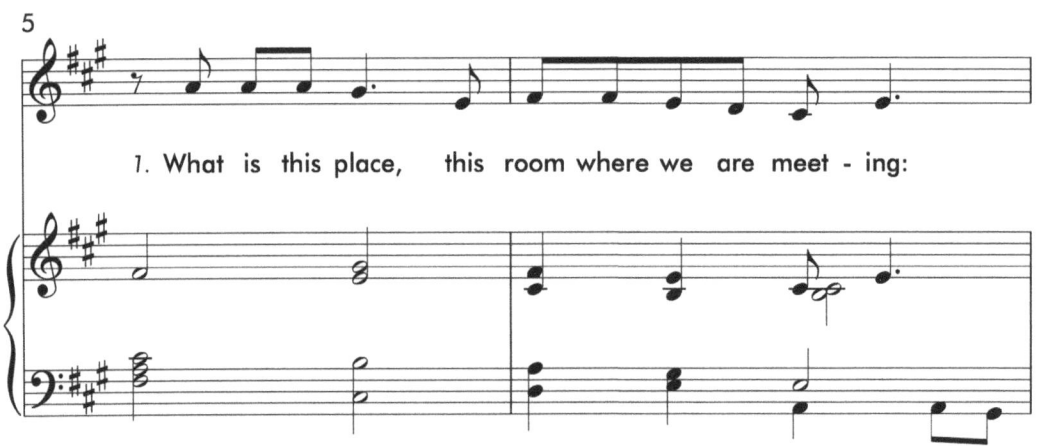

1. What is this place, this room where we are meeting:

a house for God or for the hu-man race or

Words & Music copyright © 2020 WGRG, Iona Community, Glasgow, Scotland. www.wildgoose.scot

1. What is this place,
    this room where we are meeting:
        a house for God
        or for the human race
        or both,
    since everyone bears God's image
    and shows God's trace?

2. What is this place,
    this private room for Sunday:
        a holy hall
        or very public space
        or both,
    since all life is blessed and bounded
    by God's embrace?

3. What is this place,
    this refuge from life's trouble:
        a safety net
        or temporary base
        or both,
    since all things must change 'til later
    we see God's face?

4. What is this place? –
    a canopy of grace,
        an open door,
        a storehouse of surprise,
        a taste
    of what God intends, a measure
    and gift of grace.

Written originally for the re-opening of a refurbished island church, the song poses alternative perspectives regarding the purpose of such a building.

In Christ we live

Words & Music: John L. Bell
Tune: BEGIJNHOF

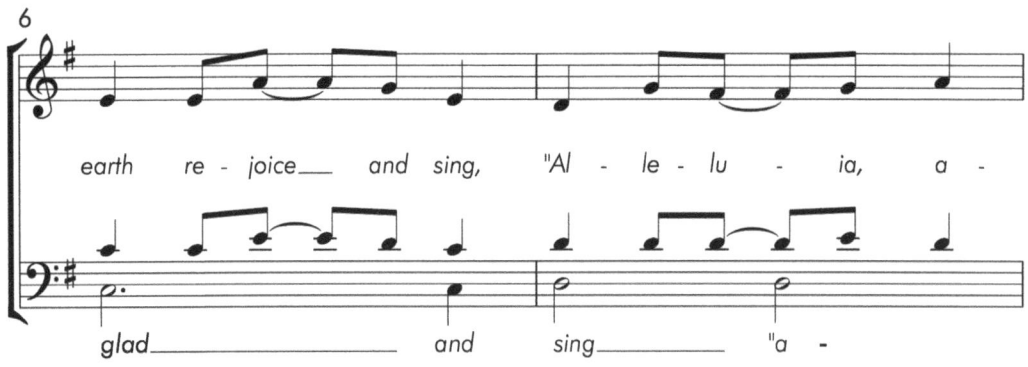

Words & Music copyright © 2011, 2020 WGRG, Iona Community, Glasgow, Scotland. www.wildgoose.scot

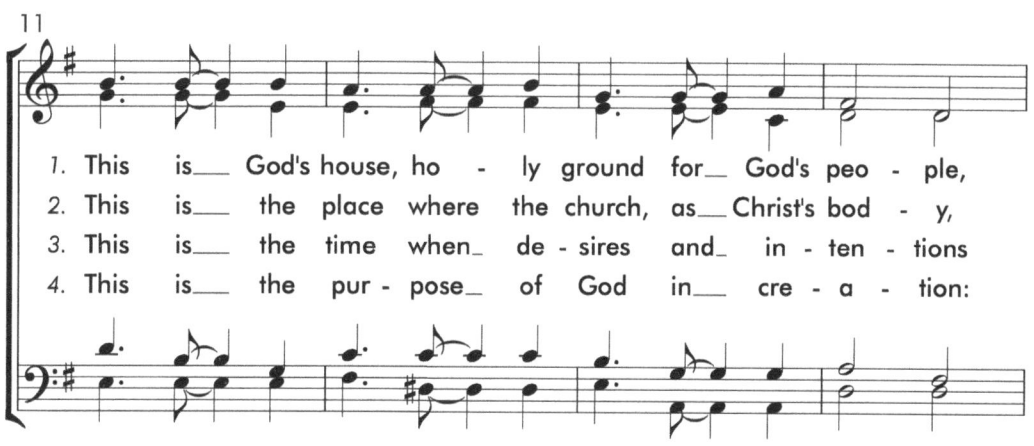

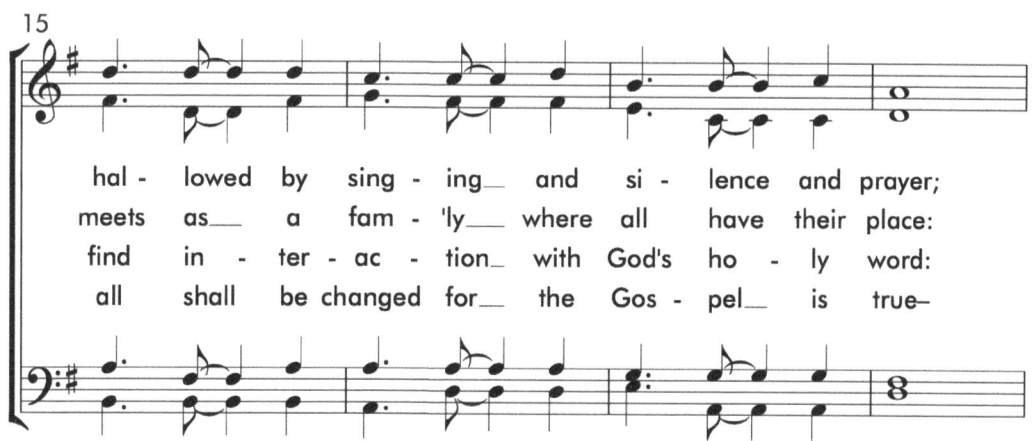

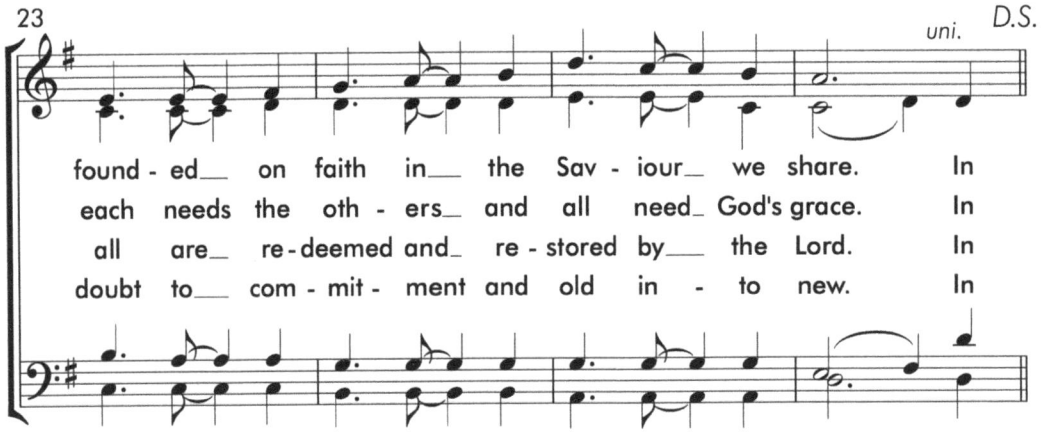

26

IN CHRIST WE LIVE AND IN CHRIST WE DIE
AND IN CHRIST WE RISE UP AGAIN.
LET HEAVEN BE GLAD AND LET EARTH REJOICE
AND SING, 'ALLELUIA, AMEN!'

1. This is God's house, holy ground for God's people,
   hallowed by singing and silence and prayer;
   blessed by the presence and power of the Spirit,
   founded on faith in the Saviour we share.

2. This is the place where the Church as Christ's body
   meets as a family where all have their place:
   stalwart and stranger, speaker and seeker –
   each needs the others and all need God's grace.

3. This is the time when desires and intentions
   find interaction with God's holy word:
   trouble and treasure, business and pleasure,
   all are redeemed and restored by the Lord.

4. This is the purpose of God in creation:
   all shall be changed for the Gospel is true –
   sickness to health, apathy to caring,
   doubt to commitment and old into new.

A more lively song, also concerning the church. There seem to be comparatively few hymns about the use and purpose of the space in which people gather to worship God.

On the recording which accompanies this book, the singers use the original ending to the tune of the verse (bar 26). However, experience has proven that congregations find the leap downwards difficult. This amended version is much easier.

A choral arrangement of this song is available. See introduction for details.

Long have you loved me

Words & Music: John L. Bell
Tune: YEARNING

1. Long have you loved me, Holy God:

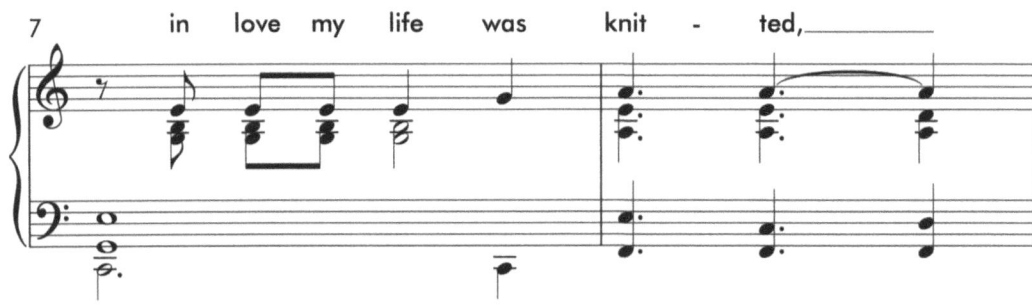

in love my life was knitted,

my self was shaped, my soul was weaned,

Words copyright © 2018, 2020 WGRG, Iona Community, Glasgow, Scotland.
Music copyright © 2020 WGRG, Iona Community, Glasgow, Scotland. www.wildgoose.scot

1. Long have you loved me, Holy God:
   in love my life was knitted,
   my self was shaped, my soul was weaned,
   my fate and future fitted.

2. Long have you loved me, Holy God,
   and freely did you fashion
   my mind, my heart, my will, my skill,
   my hesitance and passion.

3. Long have you loved me, Holy God,
   and yearned for closer bonding
   that through naught else but love, my love
   to yours might come responding.

4. Long have you loved me, Holy God;
   too long have I resisted.
   Now late I come, though from the start,
   my life in yours existed.

5. So take and make me yours, through Christ
   in whom all are perfected;
   and reap the harvest of the seed
   you sowed and resurrected.

6. Long will I love you, Holy God:
   more yet will I discover
   of who I am and who you are,
   my destiny and lover.

The image of God as Lover is prominent in the prophecies of Isaiah, Ezekiel and Hosea. And mediaeval poets employed the image with reference to Jesus, possibly encouraged by the one-time popular reading of the Song of Songs as an allegory of the relationship between Christ and the Church.

There is a balm

Words & Melody: Traditional African American
Arrangement: John L. Bell

Arrangement copyright © 2000, 2020 WGRG, Iona Community, Glasgow, Scotland. www.wildgoose.scot

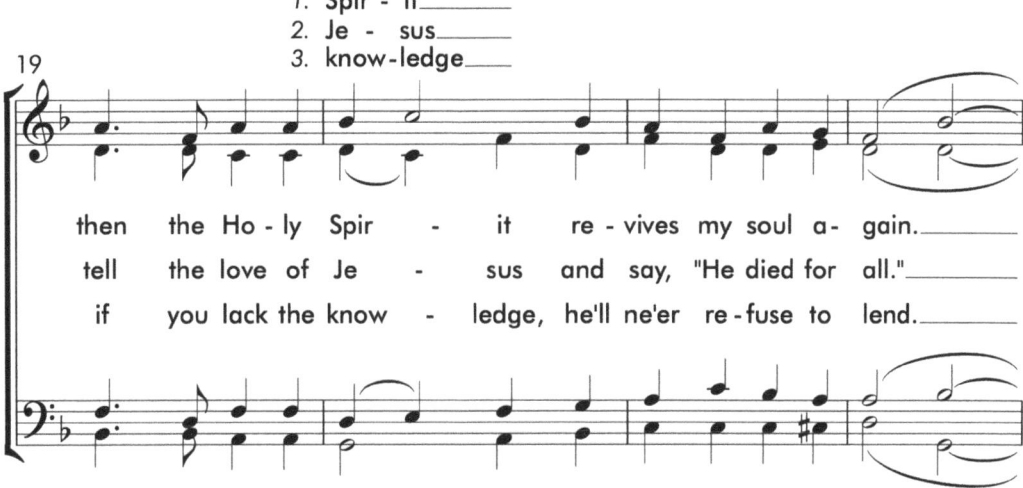

There is a balm in Gilead
to make the wounded whole;
there is a balm in Gilead
to heal the sin-sick soul.

1. Sometimes I feel discouraged
and think my work's in vain,
but then the Holy Spirit
revives my soul again.

2. If you cannot preach like Peter,
if you cannot pray like Paul,
you can tell the love of Jesus
and say, 'He died for all.'

3. Don't ever feel discouraged
for Jesus is your friend;
and if you lack the knowledge
he'll ne'er refuse to lend.

African-American spirituals, like the Psalms, as well as recording distress and anger, offer hope and solace. They have a comprehensive emotional vocabulary expressed through concise words set to memorable tunes often with few notes.

A fuller choral arrangement of this song is available. See introduction for details.

Now we are nourished

Words: John L. Bell
Melody: Ryu Hyung Sun, Korea
Arrangement: John L. Bell, Iain McLarty & others

Brightly ♩. = 68

Words copyright © 2020 WGRG, Iona Community, Glasgow, Scotland; Melody copyright © Ryu Hyung Sun
Arrangement copyright © 2020 Iain McLarty and WGRG, Iona Community, Glasgow, Scotland. www.wildgoose.scot

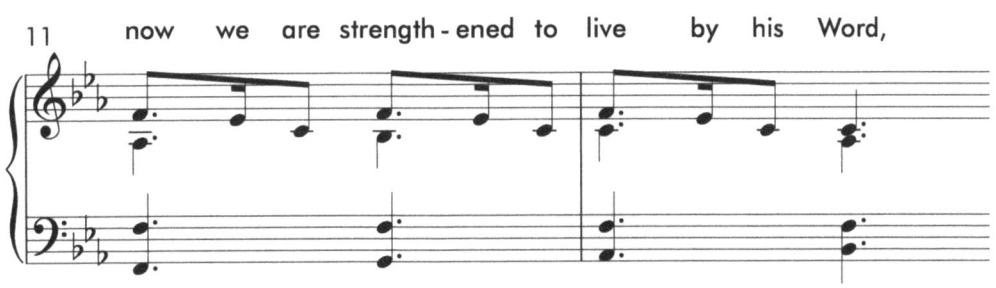

1. Now we are nourished by Jesus our Lord,
    now we are strengthened to live by his word,
    now we are summoned to love and obey,
    now we will walk in his way.

    HALLELUJAH! HALLELUJAH!
    JESUS WHO FEEDS US
    KNOWS WHERE HE LEADS US:
    NOW WE WILL WALK IN HIS WAY.

2. Now Christ has turned us from strangers to friends,
    now we affirm that his love never ends
    now for God's kingdom we'll work and we'll pray,
    now we will walk in his way.

3. Now that our journey of faith has begun,
    though some may stumble while others might run,
    Jesus precedes us into each new day;
    now we will walk in his way.

This is a delightful melody by Ryu Hyung Sun, a young Korean composer who studied with Professor Geonyong Lee, composer of the tune O So So. In keeping with many tunes from that region, it is written in a pentatonic (five-note) scale.

The introduction to the song gives it a slight ceilidh feel, celebrating the gift of the melody from Korea coming to Scotland.

In the chorus, the call and response can be between choir and congregation, women and men, or two halves of the assembly.

Lord Jesus, I'm eager to answer your call

Words: John L. Bell, derived from the Vietnamese Loi Nguyen Cau
Melody: Swedish traditional, Arrangement: John L. Bell

Prayerfully ♩ = 60

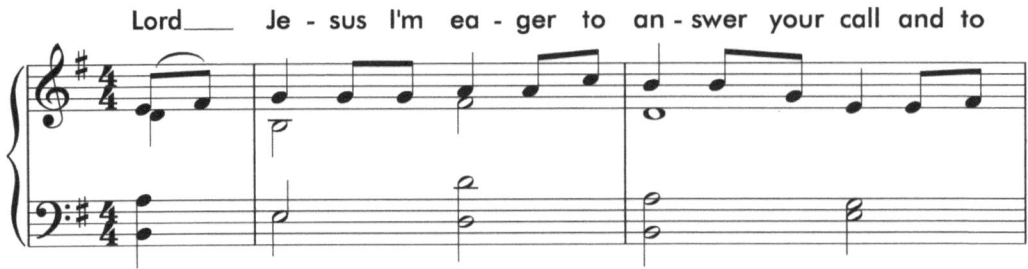

Words & Arrangement copyright © 2020 WGRG, Iona Community, Glasgow, Scotland. www.wildgoose.scot

Lord Jesus, I'm eager to answer your call
and to honour your name every day.
So take me, remake me, and call me your own
as I follow your will and your way.

This item has an unusual pedigree. It was heard by John Bell being sung by teenagers in a youth group in Ho Chi Minh City in Vietnam. In their voices, it sounded very authentic to the region, and the English text picks up the theme as translated by a young Vietnamese clergyman.

However, it has subsequently been discovered that the tune is actually a Swedish Traditional. The Swedish words usually sung to this tune have no relation to what was sung in Vietnam.

The Lord of the earth

Words: John L. Bell, based on texts of Oscar Romero
Music: John L. Bell
Tune: ROMERO

Confidently ♩. = 68

1. The Lord of the earth is a ho-ly God whose pas-sion and pur-pose are sure; and

Words & Music copyright © 2011, 2020 WGRG, Iona Community, Glasgow, Scotland. www.wildgoose.scot

1. The Lord of the earth is a holy God
   whose passion and purpose are sure,
   and those who are summoned to share God's love
   respond to the cries of the poor.
   > Alleluia! Alleluia!
   > God's *holy* purpose is sure.
   > Alleluia! Alleluia!
   > *The Lord hears* the cries of the poor.

2. The words of the prophets whom God inspired
   cannot be just silently read.
   Their summons to action must be obeyed;
   our lives should reveal what they said.
   > Alleluia! Alleluia!
   > *Prophets* cannot just be read.
   > Alleluia! Alleluia!
   > *Our lives should* reveal what they said.

3. In Jesus our Saviour we clearly see
the Church must be keen to forgo
its comfort and privilege and self-esteem
till Christ's is the lifestyle we show
   Alleluia! Alleluia!
   Privilege is what we forgo,
   Alleluia! Alleluia!
   Till Christ's is the lifestyle we show.

4. With all of creation we join to sing
in praise of the Lord of the earth
who teaches that some things must change or die,
and new life be brought to its birth.
   Alleluia! Alleluia!
   Sing to the Lord of the earth.
   Alleluia! Alleluia!
   New life must be brought to its birth.

All words are sung when following the tune.
Words in *italics* are omitted by those singing the tenor and bass parts.

The words are based on the main themes of the homilies and radio talks by the Salvadorean martyr Archbishop Oscar Romero, who was murdered in 1980 because of his opposition to the tyrannical government. He spoke for those who had no voice.

This is God's world

Words & Music: John L. Bell
Tune: GOD'S WORLD

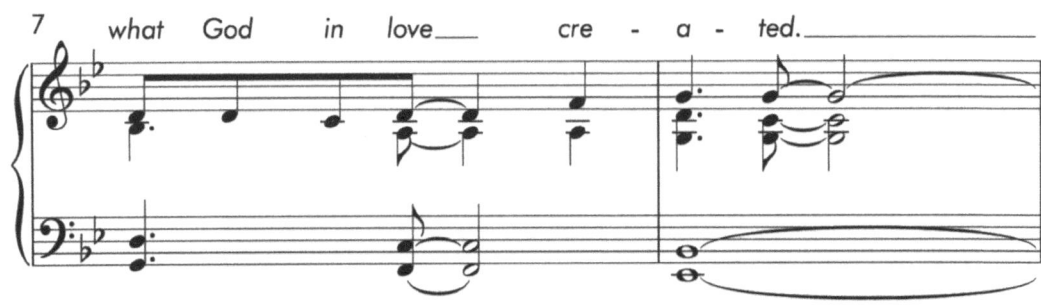

Words & Music copyright © 2008, 2020 WGRG, Iona Community, Glasgow, Scotland. www.wildgoose.scot

THIS IS GOD'S WORLD GIVEN ON LOAN;
NO OTHER EARTH SHALL BE OUR HOME.
SO LET US BLESS, HONOUR AND TEND
WHAT GOD IN LOVE CREATED.

1. Who dare disorder the song of the earth,
   silence a concert of infinite worth?
   Creation's music is meant for its Maker above,
   out of love.

2. Who dare demand or presume or require
   earth to fulfil every selfish desire?
   No wealthy nation should steal what the future will need
   out of greed.

3. Shall justice favour the powerful few,
   protecting all that they own, want and do?
   Or, under God, shall that justice be equal for all,
   great and small?

4. God grant us love that the world might survive,
   everyone prosper, the climate revive,
   let deeper listening and sharing be hallmarks of care
   everywhere.

We have many songs which admire the earth, but far fewer which recall the mandate of God to care for, indeed to be servants of, the earth. The Bible bears witness to a direct correlation between the wellbeing of humanity and the way humanity befriends or abuses the natural order.

God give them peace

Words & Music: John L. Bell
Tune: SILVER SPRAY

Pensively ♩ = 48

1. God give them peace whose hearts are seared with pain,
2. God give them peace who con-stant-ly ask why;

who've lost a friend, a lov-er or a son,
no straw to clutch, "if on-ly" they re-peat,

who sense their liv-ing is so much in vain,
and now re-hearse the words they would have said

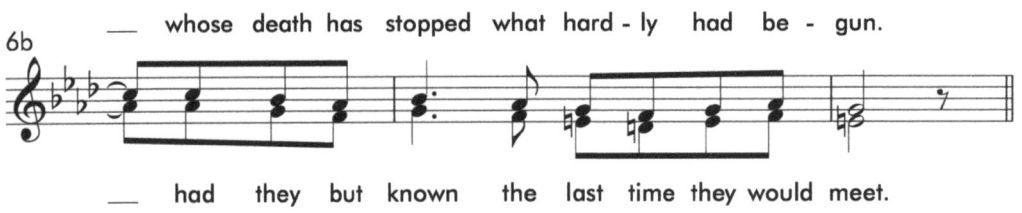

whose death has stopped what hard-ly had be-gun.
had they but known the last time they would meet.

Words & Music copyright © 2020 WGRG, Iona Community, Glasgow, Scotland. www.wildgoose.scot

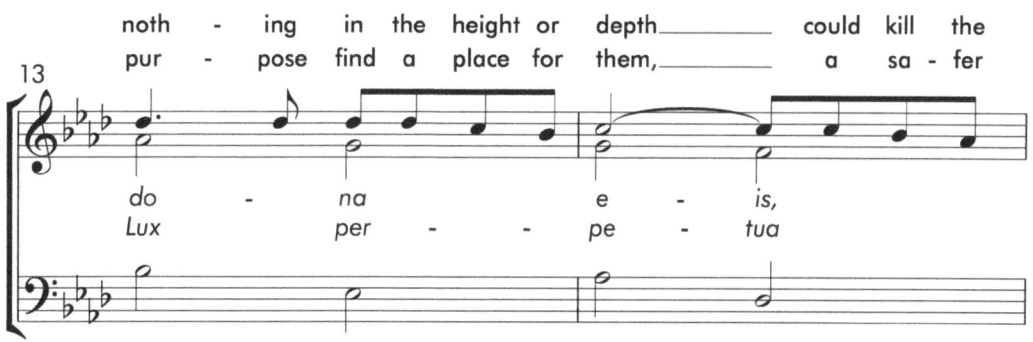
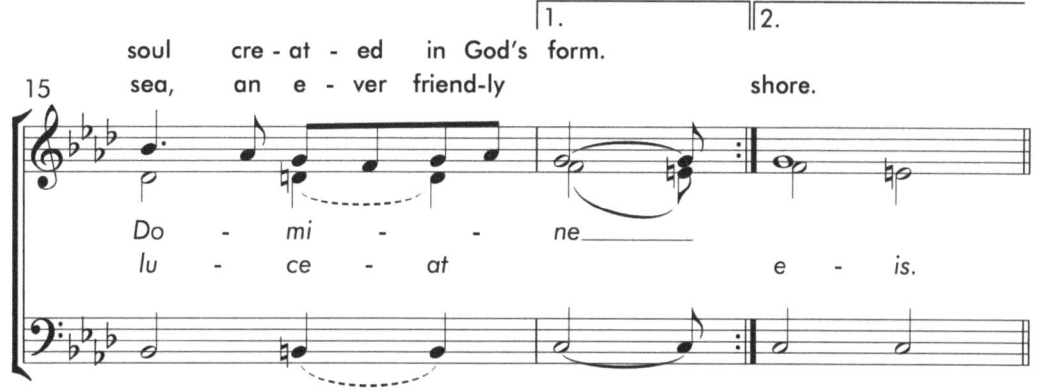

* 1. God give them peace
       whose hearts are seared with pain,
       who've lost a friend,
       a lover or a son,
       who sense their living is so much in vain,
       when death has stopped what hardly had begun.

   2. God give them peace
       who constantly ask why;
       no straw to clutch,
       'if only' they repeat,
       and now rehearse the words they would have said
       had they but known the last time they would meet.

   3. God give them peace
       but not a fragile peace,
       more like the peace
       Christ knew despite the storm,
       convinced that nothing in the height or depth
       could kill the soul created in God's form.

   4. God give them peace
       whose voices now are still,
       whose touch is gone,
       whose laughter rings no more.
       In your great purpose find a place for them,
       a safer sea, an ever friendly shore. Amen.

Requiem æternam dona eis, Domine. (Eternal rest give to them, O Lord.)
Lux perpetua luceat eis. (Let perpetual light shine upon them.)

One night in 1998, four young men – three from the island of Iona – were drowned at sea as a result of the boat in which they were sailing being capsized by a freak wave. This was a great loss to the local community which had few boys of their age among its less than one hundred permanent residents.

The song, as recorded, has verse one for a soloist or sopranos, verse two for a duet or sopranos and contraltos, and uses four part harmony in verses three and four.

This song may be of use in times of bereavement.
*To ensure inclusivity, the last four lines of verse one may be changed thus:

>who've lost a child,
>a lover or a friend,
>who sense their living is so much in vain
>when death has brought such an untimely end.

We are coming, Lord, to the table

Words & Music: Sierra Leone traditional
Transcription & Arrangement: Greg Scheer

Prayerfully ♩ = 100

We are co-ming, Lord, to the ta-ble.

We are co-ming, Lord, to the ta-ble.

1. With the gift of bread, we are com-ing, Lord.
2. To re-ceive the bread, we are com-ing, Lord.

Oh, sing it o-ver:

With the gift of wine, we are co-ming, Lord.
To re-ceive the wine, we are co-ming, Lord.

Arrangement copyright © 2008 Greg Scheer.

We are coming, Lord, to the table.
We are coming, Lord, to the table.

With the gift of bread, we are coming, Lord.
With the gift of wine, we are coming, Lord.

Oh, sing it over.
Oh, we are coming, Lord.
We offer you the gift of bread.
Oh, we are coming, Lord.
We offer you the gift of wine.
Oh, we are coming, Lord.
Oh, sing it over.
Oh, we are coming, Lord.

We are coming, Lord, to the table.
We are coming, Lord, to the table.

To receive the bread, we are coming, Lord.
To receive the wine, we are coming, Lord.

Oh, sing it over.
Oh, we are coming, Lord.
We're coming to receive the bread.
Oh, we are coming, Lord.
We're coming to receive the wine.
Oh, we are coming, Lord.
Oh, sing it over.
Oh, we are coming, Lord.

The repetition in this song makes it ideally suited for singing as the bread and wine for holy communion are being presented. It can be sung as many times as necessary. It works well with a simple percussion accompaniment which can build energy as the song progresses.

Within the circle of your friends

Words: John L. Bell
Tune: REPTON, C.H.H. Parry (1848-1918)
Arrangement: Iain McLarty & others

Words copyright © 2018, 2020 WGRG, Iona Community, Glasgow, Scotland. www.wildgoose.scot
Arrangement copyright © 2020 Iain McLarty.

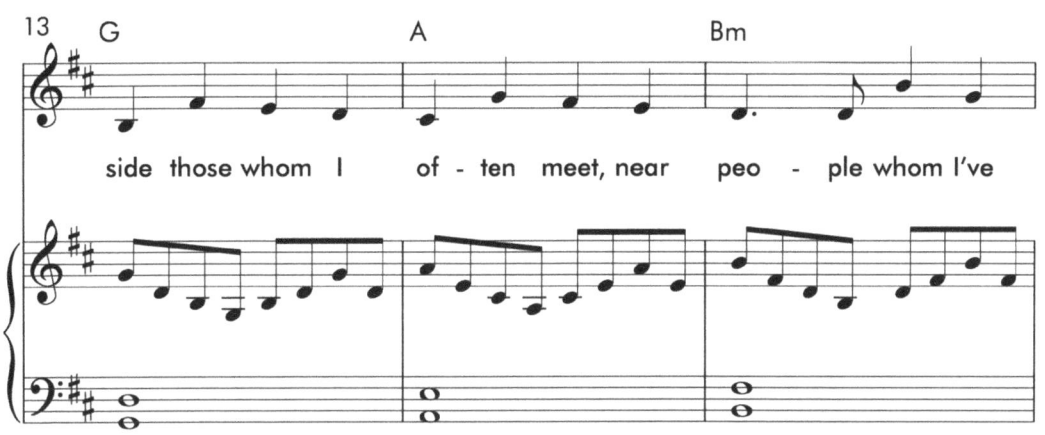
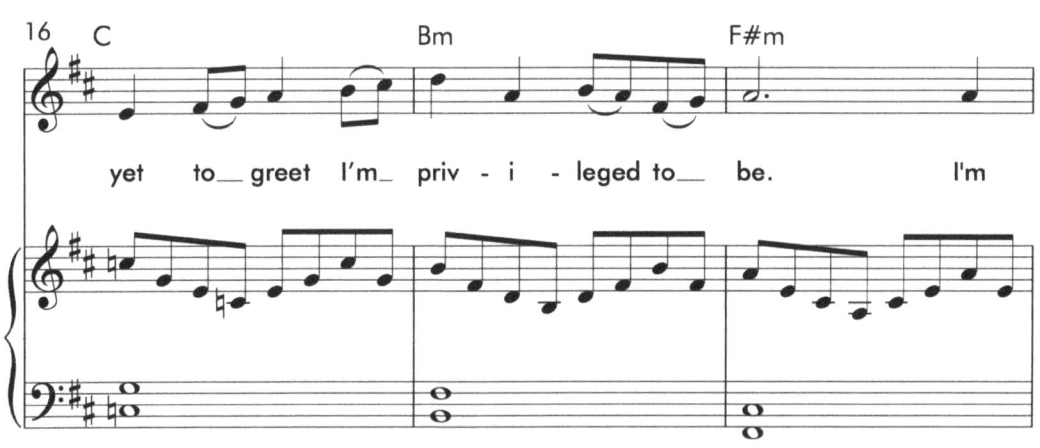
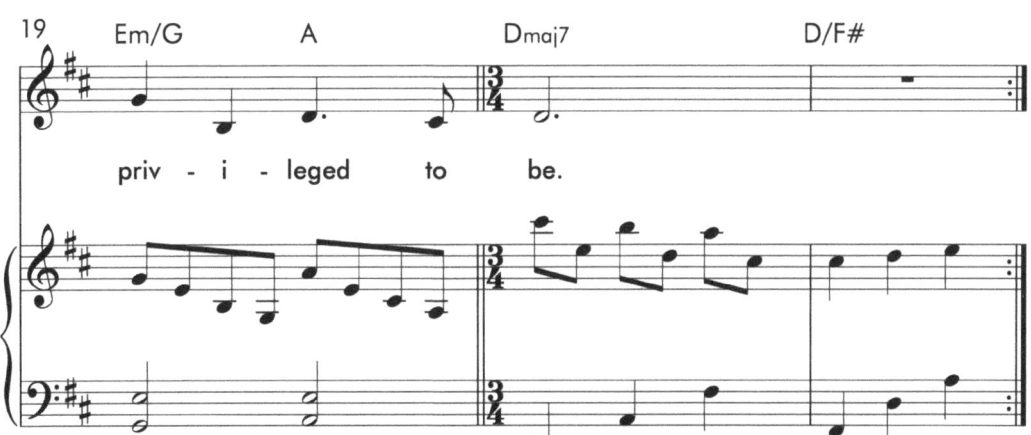

1. Within the circle of your friends,
   you found a place for me.
   Beside those whom I often meet,
   near people whom I've yet to greet
   I'm privileged to be.

2. Within your commonwealth of love,
   you found a place for me
   to listen, heal, disturb or care,
   seek words to sing, find truth to share,
   let life be full and free.

3. Around the table you prepare,
   you found a place for me
   where, breaking bread and pouring wine,
   you tell us all, 'This means you're mine,
   and mine you'll always be.'

4. Now brother, servant, Saviour, Lord,
   I make a place for you.
   Called to your feast, among your friends,
   and keen to live as God intends,
   I come to be made new.

This is a communion hymn set to the well-known tune Repton, commonly sung to *Dear Lord and Father of Mankind*. Here it is presented with an alternative accompaniment more suited to piano or guitar than the original organ version.

God and parent of all people

Words & Arrangement: John L. Bell
Tune: CRADLE SONG, James Scott Skinner (1843-1927)

Words copyright © 2018, 2020 WGRG, Iona Community, Glasgow, Scotland.
Arrangement copyright © 2020 WGRG, Iona Community, Glasgow, Scotland. www.wildgoose.scot

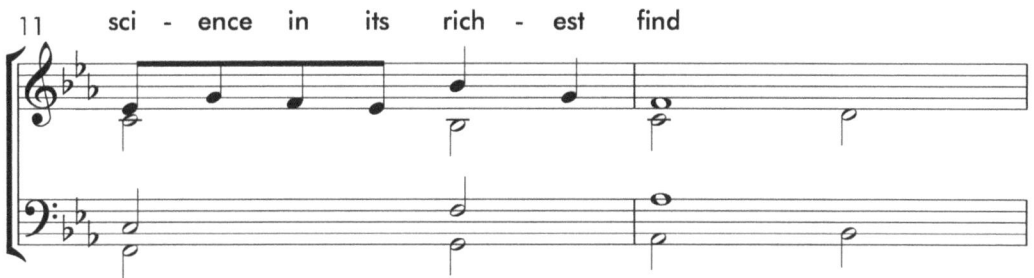
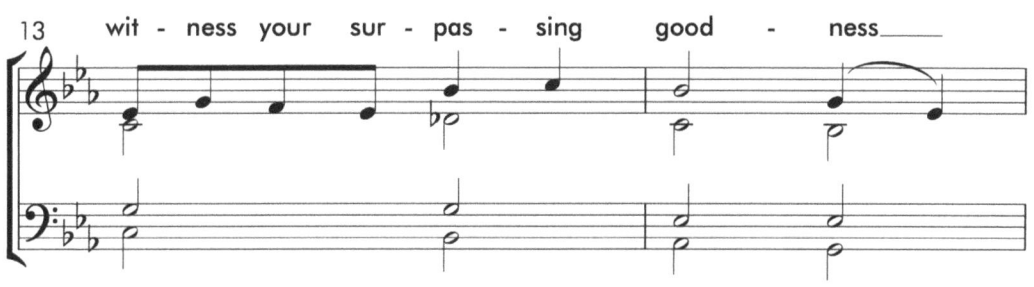

1. God and parent of all people,
   maker of both heaven and earth,
   praise and gratitude we offer
   for the world you brought to birth.
   Nature in its finest clothing,
   science in its richest find
   witness your surpassing goodness,
   meant to nourish humankind.

2. Jesus Christ, eternal Saviour,
   once a child on Mary's breast,
   born to save the saint and sinner,
   destined to reveal God's best,
   you found praise in children's voices,
   you blessed babies by your touch;
   you declare for every infant
   how God loves each one so much.

3. Holy Spirit, sent among us,
   binding earth to heaven above,
   you inspire that selfless beauty
   seen where people share their love.
   For the fruits of human passion
   in the womb, the world, the heart,
   we express, as Christ's own family,
   gratitude in every part.

4. God, be present in our worship,
   welcoming the one we bring;
   as we baptise, through your Spirit
   seal the grace of which we sing.
   Let our prayers and heaven's intention
   hallow water, sign and vow;
   bless this child whose life is offered
   to embody your life now.

This hymn for infant baptism is set to a beautiful melody by the Scottish fiddler James Scott Skinner (1843–1927).

Where there is more than one baby being baptised, the penultimate line should be changed from 'bless this child' to 'bless each child'.

God loved the world so much

Words & Arrangement: John L. Bell
Tune: WONDROUS LOVE, North American traditional

Words copyright © 2018, 2020 WGRG, Iona Community, Glasgow, Scotland.
Arrangement copyright © 2020 WGRG, Iona Community, Glasgow, Scotland. www.wildgoose.scot

1. God loved the world so much – this we know, this we know;
   God loved the world so much – this we know;
   God loved the world so much, the world and not the church,
   that Christ came into touch, into time, into view
   declaring he would make all things new.

2. When people heard his voice, all were changed, all were changed;
   when people heard his voice, all were changed;
   when people heard his voice, some rankled, some rejoiced:
   he came to vindicate what was right, what was right,
   expose deceit and share truth and light.

3. The wretched of the earth he embraced, he embraced,
   the wretched of the earth he embraced;
   the sick and sad and poor he led to heaven's door,
   and there, beside the fearful and flawed, overawed,
   they felt the warmth and welcome of God.

4. On earth itself he sowed seeds of peace, seeds of peace;
on earth itself he sowed seeds of peace;
and for the world, its health, its wisdom and its wealth,
he broke the bread of heaven and he shared it around
that justice might become common ground.

5. Shall we who bear his name stay the same, stay the same?
Shall we who bear his name stay the same?
Or shall we turn our face towards a different place
and, hearing words of grace meant for all, meant for all,
respond to Jesus' promise and call?

6. To God we give ourselves, body, mind, heart and soul;
we give our body, mind, heart and soul.
O Jesus, now instil a passion for your will
to love all people and, in our care of the earth,
walk in your way and cherish our worth.

This is a magnificent North American tune which is commonly associated with the text *What wondrous love is this?* It is the kind of melody which, whether sung unaccompanied in unison or given full orchestral treatment, always stubbornly retains its character.

Not all verses need be sung. Verses 3, 4 and 6 may be omitted.

* The asterisk in bar two indicates the point of entry for singing the tune as a round.
This would probably be best with the last verse.

Go, heal the sick

Paraphrase of Matthew 10 & Music: John L. Bell
Tune: RAMIREZ

With enthusiasm ♩ = 120

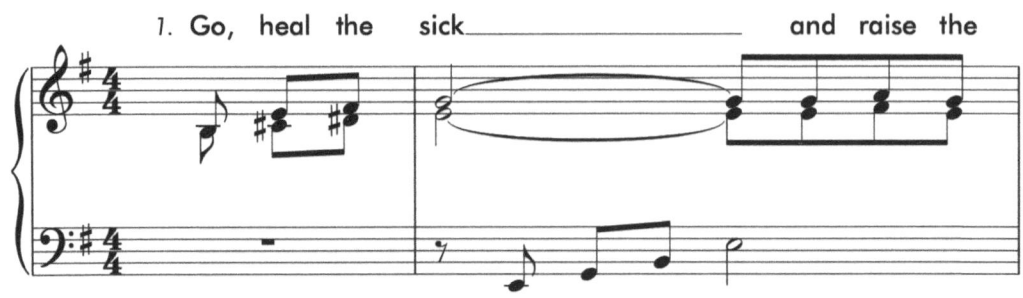

1. Go, heal the sick and raise the

dead, restore the broken, banish ev-'ry

de-mon; and do all this with-out a

charge, for li-be-ra-tion comes free-ly from God.

Paraphrase & Music copyright © 2020 WGRG, Iona Community, Glasgow, Scotland. www.wildgoose.scot

1. Go, heal the sick and raise the dead,
   restore the broken, banish every demon;
   and do all this without a charge
   for liberation comes freely from God.

   THIS IS OUR COMMISSION, THIS IS JESUS' OWN WORD,
   THIS THE EXPECTATION OF OUR SAVIOUR AND LORD;
   THIS IS WHAT HE ASKS OF THOSE WHO FOLLOW HIS WAY,
   AND WHO TAKE TO HEART ALL THEY HEAR HIM SAY.
   HEAVEN IS NOT AFTERLIFE UNLESS IT IS NOW,
   GOD IS FOUND IN SILENCE AND IN SUFFERING AND ROW;
   UNDISTURBED DISCIPLESHIP IS NOT TRUE TO FORM,
   JESUS' PEACE IS FOUND IN THE STORM.

2. Forget your purse, forget your pack,
   one change of clothes is all you will be needing.
   I send you out like sheep to wolves;
   be wise as serpents and gentle as doves.

3. Be on your guard when brought to court
   to speak before the merciless and mighty.
   But take no thought for what you'll say;
   the words will come when God's moment is right.

4. You must not think I came to soothe;
   I brought a sword to hasten provocation.
   If you confess my name on earth,
   I'll mention yours in the presence of God.

5. No one is fit to come with me
   who does not lift the cross and follow after.
   If, for my sake, you lose your life,
   I will restore it with honour and love.

The words are a paraphrase of verses in Matthew chapter 10, where Jesus, in sending out his disciples, does not give some kind of catch-all pious blessing, but is quite specific regarding what their signature in the world should be.

Murassala

Words & Music: as taught by Beatrice Mukhtar Mamuzi, South Sudan

Copyright © All Saints' Cathedral, Juba, South Sudan

Murassala nina kulumurassala.
Murassala nina kulumurassala.
Murassala nina kulumurassala.
Nina kulumurassala le Yesu.

Shukuru Alaa nina kulumurassala.
Shukuru Alaa nina kulumurassala.
Shukuru Alaa nina kulumurassala.
Nina kulumurassala le Yesu.

Hallelujah! Nina kulumurassala.
Hallelujah! Nina kulumurassala.
Hallelujah! Nina kulumurassala.
Nina kulumurassala le Yesu.

A singable English text to this song is given below. In its original language it refers to the singers being messengers or ambassadors.

1. Sing praise to God! We will follow where Jesus calls. *(three times)*
   We will follow where Jesus calls every day.

2. Hallelujah! We will follow where Jesus calls. *(three times)*
   We will follow where Jesus calls every day.

This song from South Sudan reminds us that we are all called to mission and makes for a joyful sending song. The Arabic lyrics are easiest to learn when taught in rhythm with a light syncopation and then adding the melody afterwards.

We often imagine African songs being sung a cappella with hand percussion but nowadays guitars and keyboards will often be added.

Canticle of the turning

Paraphrase of Luke 1, Adaptation & Arrangement: Rory Cooney
Tune: STAR OF THE COUNTY DOWN, Irish traditional

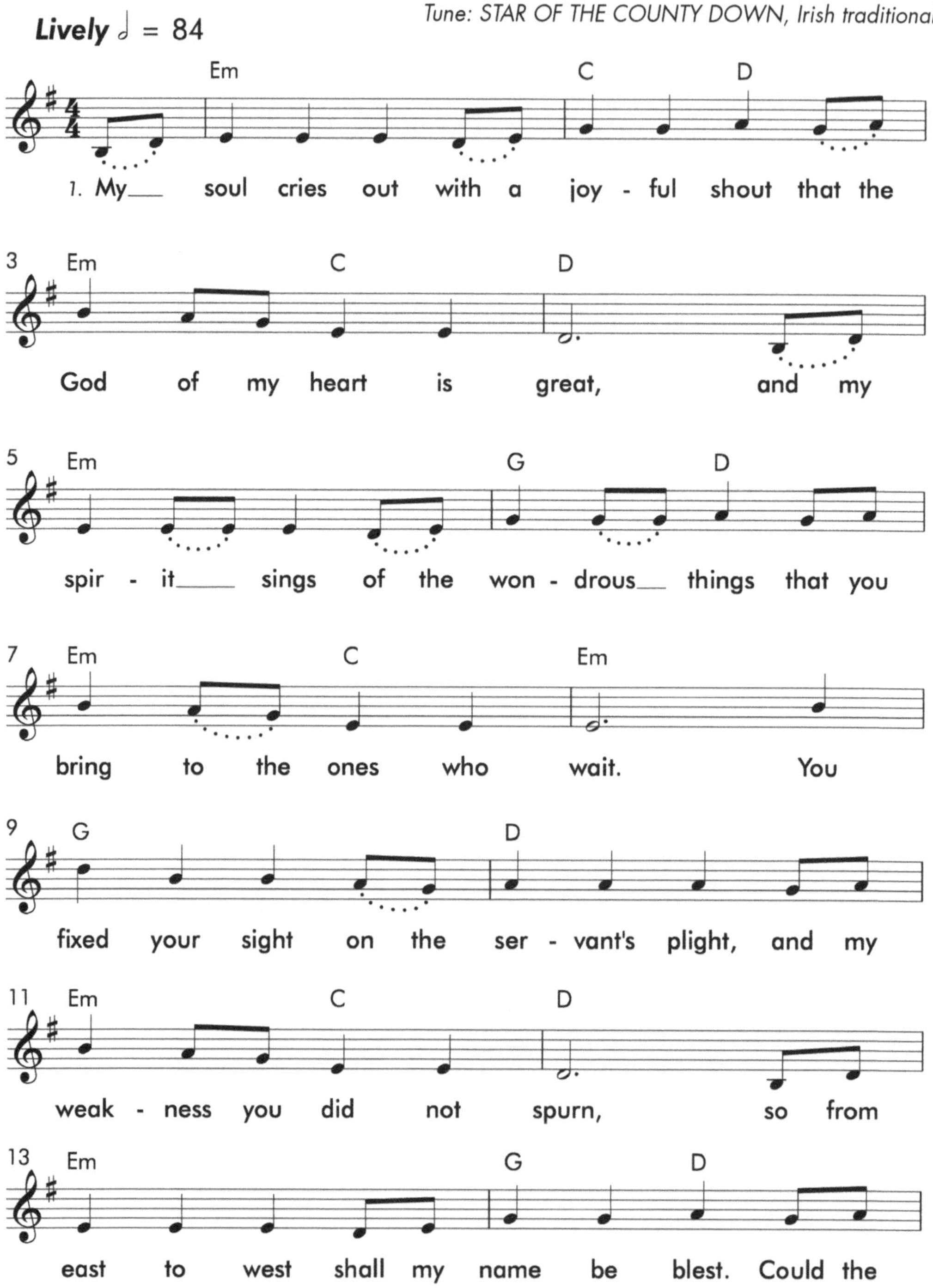

Lively ♩ = 84

1. My soul cries out with a joy-ful shout that the God of my heart is great, and my spir-it sings of the won-drous things that you bring to the ones who wait. You fixed your sight on the ser-vant's plight, and my weak-ness you did not spurn, so from east to west shall my name be blest. Could the

Copyright © 1990 GIA Publications, Inc. All rights reserved.

79

1. My soul cries out with a joyful shout that the God of my heart is great,
   and my spirit sings of the wondrous things that you bring to the ones who wait.
   You fixed your sight on your servant's plight and my weakness you did not spurn
   so from east to west shall my name be blest. Could the world be about to turn?

   MY HEART SHALL SING OF THE DAY YOU BRING.
   LET THE FIRES OF YOUR JUSTICE BURN.
   WIPE AWAY ALL TEARS, FOR THE DAWN DRAWS NEAR,
   AND THE WORLD IS ABOUT TO TURN.

2. Though I am small, my God my all, you work great things in me,
   and your mercy will last from the depths of the past to the end of the age to be.
   Your very name puts the proud to shame; and to those who would for you yearn,
   you will show your might, put the strong to flight, for the world is about to turn.

3. From the halls of power to the fortress tower, not a stone will be left on stone.
   Let the king beware for your justice tears every tyrant from his throne.
   The hungry poor shall weep no more, for the food they can never earn;
   there are tables spread, every mouth be fed, for the world is about to turn.

4. Though the nations rage from age to age, we remember who holds us fast:
   God's mercy must deliver us from the conqueror's crushing grasp.
   This saving word that our forebears heard is the promise which holds us bound,
   'til the spear and rod can be crushed by God who is turning the world around.

The Magnificat, as it appears in Luke Chapter 1, is the source of this text which, allied to the lively Irish folk tune, enables a sense of Mary being an ordinary country girl, something which confected choral renderings seldom do. Rory Cooney is an American with Irish roots who is a full time director of music in a Catholic Community in Barrington, Illinois.

If accompanied, a guitar and flute are far better than a keyboard.

I lie down with God

Words: Ancient Celtic Prayer
Music: John L. Bell
Tune: GRAHAM

*Words transcribed and translated by Alexander Carmichael (1832-1912),
Carmina Gadelica, Floris Books, Edinburgh 1992.
Music copyright © 2020 WGRG, Iona Community, Glasgow, Scotland. www.wildgoose.scot*

I lie down with God, and God lies down with me.
I lie down with Jesus Christ, and Christ lies down with me.
I lie down with the Holy Spirit, and the Holy Spirit lies down with me.
God and Jesus and the Holy Spirit,
all three with me.

The author of this text is unknown, but it appears in *Carmina Gadelica*, a collection of poems and prayers handed down in the oral tradition of the Gaelic speaking regions of Scotland. The texts were collected and translated by Alexander Carmichael (1832-1912), a civil servant who devoted himself to conserving the wisdom and spirituality of a culture and language under constant threat.

Ideally the first phrase in lines one to three should be sung by a solo voice, or by the sopranos alone.

Alphabetical index of first lines

16	All people living on the earth
70	Go, heal the sick and raise the dead
62	God and parent of all people
50	God give them peace whose hearts are seared with pain
66	God loved the world so much – this we know, this we know
12	Hallelujah! Hallelujah!
82	I lie down with God, and God lies down with me
24	In Christ we live and in Christ we die
28	Long have you loved me, Holy God
38	Lord Jesus, I'm eager to answer your call
76	Murassala nina kulumurassala
78	My soul cries out with a joyful shout that the God of my heart is great
34	Now we are nourished by Jesus our Lord
40	The Lord of the earth is a holy God
30	There is a balm in Gilead
24	This is God's house, holy ground for God's people
46	This is God's world given on loan
12	This is the day that God has made
54	We are coming, Lord, to the table
20	What is this place, this room where we are meeting?
46	Who dare disorder the song of the earth?
58	Within the circle of your friends

The Iona Community

The Iona Community is:
- An ecumenical movement of people from different walks of life and different traditions in the Christian Church
- Committed to the gospel of Jesus Christ, and to following where that leads, even into the unknown
- Engaged together, and with people of goodwill across the world, in acting, reflecting and praying for justice, peace and the integrity of creation
- Convinced that the inclusive community we seek must be embodied in the community we practise

Together with our staff, we are responsible for:
- Our islands residential centres of Iona Abbey, the MacLeod Centre on Iona, and Camas Adventure Centre on the Ross of Mull

and in Glasgow:
- The administration of the Community
- Our work with young people
- Our publishing house, Wild Goose Publications
- Our association in the revitalising of worship with the Wild Goose Resource Group

The Iona Community was founded in Glasgow in 1938 by George MacLeod, minister, visionary and prophetic witness for peace, in the context of the poverty and despair of the Depression. Its original task of rebuilding the monastic ruins of Iona Abbey became a sign of hopeful rebuilding of community in Scotland and beyond. Today, we are about 280 Members, mostly in Britain, and 1500 Associate Members, with 1400 Friends worldwide. Together and apart, 'we follow the light we have, and pray for more light'.

For information on the Iona Community contact:
The Iona Community, Suite 9, Fairfield
1048 Govan Road, Glasgow G51 4XS, Scotland
Tel: **+44 (0)141 429 7281**
E-mail: **admin@iona.org.uk**
Web: **www.iona.org.uk**

For enquiries about visiting Iona, please contact:
Iona Abbey, Isle of Iona, Argyll PA76 6SN, UK.
Tel: **+44 (0)1681 700404**
E-mail: **enquiries@iona.org.uk**

Wild Goose Publications

The publishing house of the Iona Community, established in the Celtic Christian tradition of Saint Columba, produces books, CDs and digital downloads on:

- holistic spirituality
- social justice
- political and peace issues
- healing
- innovative approaches to worship
- songs for worship, including the work of the Wild Goose Resource Group
- material for meditation and reflection

For more information, please contact us at:
Wild Goose Publications,
The Iona Community, Suite 9, Fairfield
1048 Govan Road, Glasgow G51 4XS, Scotland

Tel: **+44 (0)141 429 7281**
E-mail: **admin@ionabooks.com**
Web: **www.ionabooks.com** (details of products and online sales)

The Wild Goose Resource Group

The Wild Goose Resource Group is an expression of the Iona Community's commitment to the renewal of public worship. Based in Glasgow, the WGRG has two resource workers, John Bell and Jo Love, who lead workshops, seminars and events throughout Britain and abroad. They are supported by Gail Ullrich, the Group's administrator.

The task of the WGRG has been to develop and identify new methods and materials to enable the revitalisation of congregational song, prayer and liturgy. Songs and liturgical material have been translated and used in many countries across the world as well as being frequently broadcast on radio and television. All music in this collection has been recorded by the Wild Goose Collective — an ad hoc assortment of singers associated with the Resource Group.

If you would like to find out more about ways to support the WGRG financially, please contact:

Wild Goose Resource Group,
The Iona Community,
Suite 9, Fairfield
1048 Govan Road
Glasgow G51 4XS, Scotland
Tel: **+44 (0)141 429 7281**
E-mail: **wildgoose@wildgoose.scot**

Web: **www.wildgoose.scot**

Also from the Wild Goose Resource Group ...

Known Unknowns: 100 contemporary texts to common tunes
John L. Bell & Graham Maule
The 100 texts in this volume represent a wide gamut of subject matter, from psalm paraphrases to songs about ecology, abuse, money, depression, and delight. Almost all of the tunes used can be found in any hymnal. The 'Knowns' are the familiar tunes to which the texts are set. The 'Unknowns' are the texts, some of which have never been published, and some that were previously published with original tunes, thus perhaps remaining somewhat 'Unknown'. These hymns are put together especially for the kind of churches the Wild Goose Resource Group wants to encourage—churches where there is no musician, churches where there is a reluctance to sing new songs, or churches where the praise of God has been kept separate from the concerns of the world. Book: ISBN 9781849525671

The Truth That Sets Us Free: Biblical songs for worship
John L. Bell & Wild Goose Collective
A collection of longer songs from John L. Bell & the Wild Goose Resource Group. As with previous albums, these are not songs written for an instant market, but songs that have done the rounds, been road-tested at home and abroad, and have proved their worth. Coming from places as far apart as Singapore, Mozambique and Glasgow, the only common thread is in the title. The 'truth that sets us free' – a quotation from St. John's Gospel – is recognised in songs about healing, racism, winter and Holy Communion as well as in settings of psalms and other biblical texts. Book: ISBN 9781849522304; CD: ISBN 9781849522403

We Walk His Way: Short songs for worship, Vol.3
John L. Bell & Wild Goose Collective
The third in the series of wee songs that have proved to be hugely popular and useful in English-speaking countries. Several of the songs have also been translated into other European languages. Some shorter songs bear continual repetition for meditation or as an accompaniment to liturgical action; some may be interspersed with prayer or scripture reading, some – like the Sanctus – have a particular place in the celebration of Holy Communion. But all, being short, are memorable. They can link us to the greater universal church; they may provide for our memory words which are worth keeping; and they may be the means whereby people who have never sung in harmony get a foot up that ladder. Book: ISBN 9781905010554; CD: ISBN 9781905010424

I Will Not Sing Alone: Songs for the seasons of love
John L. Bell & Wild Goose Collective
A deliberately eclectic collection of words & music from different ages, fused in contemporary arrangements. The seventeen songs include exclamations of praise, meditative reflections on the love of God, laments for the loss of a child and for countries at war. Book: ISBN 9781901557916; CD: ISBN 9781901557893

10 Things They Never Told Me About Jesus: A beginner's guide to a larger Christ
John L. Bell

Not another book about what we already know, but one about what we overlook. Here, John Bell explores facets of the personal life, relationships and ministry of Jesus which are seldom the stuff of preaching or conversation, but which are all rooted in the Gospels and are necessary if we are to be freed from the passive stereotypes which still dominate thinking about Christ. Book: ISBN 9781905010608

The Singing Thing: A case for congregational song
John L. Bell

One of the world's experts on congregational song writes for those who want to encourage others to sing or sing better. He offers ten persuasive answers to the question 'Why do we sing?' Each answer is explored with a wealth of practical insight born of the author's thirty years of experience in this field. Book: ISBN 9781901557282

The Singing Thing Too: Enabling congregations to sing
John L. Bell

The second of John Bell's books dealing with the case for congregational song. Here he deals with the 'how to' issues; the techniques of teaching songs to congregations and groups. Describing this process as 'an exercise in communicating truth through personality', drawing on both his own and colleagues' extensive and devoted practical experience, John crystallises the distinctive WGRG approach which has inspired and enthused countless folk to sing, often despite their own misgivings, over the last thirty years. Book: ISBN 9781905010325

RESOURCE BOOKS

Cloth for the Cradle (Book), Wild Goose Worship Group; ISBN 9781901557015
He Was In The World (Book), John L. Bell; ISBN 9780947988708
Jesus & Peter (Book), John L. Bell & Graham Maule; ISBN 9781901557176
Present On Earth (Book), Wild Goose Worship Group; ISBN 9781901557640
Stages On The Way (Book), Wild Goose Worship Group; ISBN 9781901557114
Wee Worship Book, A (4th Incarnation) (Book), John L. Bell & Mairi Munro; ISBN 9781901557190
Wee Worship Book, A (5th Incarnation) (Book), John L. Bell & Graham Maule; ISBN 9781849523226

Order these and more online at www.ionabooks.com or www.wildgoose.scot